MODERN WORLD NATIONS

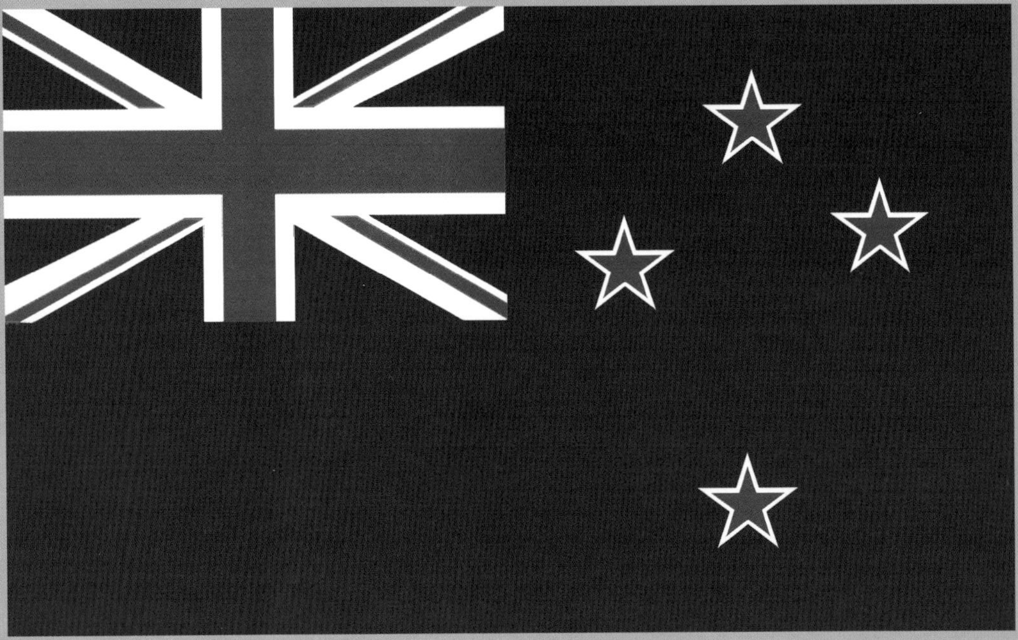

New Zealand

Carol Ann Gillespie
Grove City College

Series Consulting Editor
Charles F. Gritzner
South Dakota State University

CHELSEA HOUSE
PUBLISHERS
An imprint of Infobase Publishing

Frontispiece: Flag of New Zealand

Cover: Steam rises from Champagne Pool at Wai-o-tapu Thermal Park on New Zealand's North Island.

New Zealand

Copyright © 2002, Updated Edition 2005 by Infobase Publishing

Chelsea House
An imprint of Infobase Publishing
132 West 31st Street
New York NY 10001

ISBN-10: 0-7910-8708-5
ISBN-13: 978-0-7910-8708-4

Library of Congress Cataloging-in-Publication Data

CIP applied for ISBN 0-7910-8708-5

Chelsea House books are available at special discounts when purchased in bulk quantities for businesses, associations, institutions, or sales promotions. Please call our Special Sales Department in New York at (212) 967-8800 or (800) 322-8755.

You can find Chelsea House on the World Wide Web at http://www.chelseahouse.com

Series and cover design by Takeshi Takahashi

Printed in China

Nordica 21C 10 9 8 7 6 5 4 3 2

This book is printed on acid-free paper.

Table of Contents

New Zealand

For over 1,000 years New Zealand has been known as the Land of the Long White Cloud.

Introducing
New Zealand

W hen the Polynesian navigator Kupe came across New
Zealand in about 950 A.D., he called it Aotearoa—the
Land of the Long White Cloud. This name aptly
described the frequent and impressive fog banks created by thick
clouds and snow-capped mountain peaks. New Zealand is a land
of lofty mountains and shimmering, glacially scoured mountain
lakes. It is a country blessed with a mild and pleasant climate and
ample rainfall evenly distributed throughout the year. New
Zealand has no snakes or dangerous wild animals, which makes it
the ideal spot for an outdoor vacation.

New Zealand is a country with many of the natural splendors
of the United States combined in an area the size of Colorado. In
New Zealand, rivers plunge over skyscraper-tall waterfalls, and the
surrounding waters swarm with whales, dolphins, and penguins.

Giant kauri trees reach skyward, and glaciers slowly melt down steep mountainsides to reach the lush midlatitude rain forests below. Only 28 percent of New Zealand is still forested, with most of the land having been cleared for cropland and pasture. In fact, New Zealand has 11 times as many sheep and nearly three times as many cattle as it has people!

New Zealand owes its very existence to undersea mountain building. The country has two main islands: North Island and South Island. The active volcanic peaks and geothermal features of the North Island, in particular, reveal the country's fiery origins. As in Australia, New Zealand's isolation offered opportunities for the development of unique plant and animal species: Eighty-five percent of the country's native trees and plants are found nowhere else on earth. Bats are New Zealand's only native land mammals, while tuatara reptiles and kiwi birds are examples of New Zealand's unique wildlife diversity.

New Zealand is a land of fascinating cultures. The indigenous Maori, with their elaborate facial and bodily tattoos, once greeted European explorers with curses and snarling tongues. These days the Maori take out their aggressions on the rugby field, where the descendants of the English settlers cheer them on. The Maori and Samoan players are central to New Zealand's world dominance in rugby. At the start of a game, the players perform the Maori war dance, the *haka*, to arouse feelings of aggression. Many New Zealand players are Samoan in origin. Samoans are Polynesians, and Polynesians are noted for their size, strength, and skill in athletic games.

Because New Zealand lies in the Southern Hemisphere, the seasons are the reverse of those in the Northern Hemisphere. Our summer is their winter, and the farther north one travels in New Zealand, the warmer it gets. However, temperatures usually are very pleasant and range between 40 and 70 degrees F (4 to 21 degrees C) year-round.

New Zealand's first settlers, the Maori, named the kiwi bird for the sound of its call: *kiwi-kiwi-kiwi!* This flightless bird,

Adopted by all New Zealanders as their national emblem, the kiwi is hardly a typical bird. This brown kiwi chick may have been raised in captivity so that its chances of survival in the wild are enhanced.

about the size of a domestic hen, has an extremely long beak and plumage that is more like hair than feathers. New Zealanders adopted this nocturnal, flightless, and very delightful bird as their national emblem.

Old Maori customs, such as the *pukana*, or snarling tongue, have survived into the 21st century.

New Zealanders themselves are also referred to as Kiwis. This probably dates back to World War I, when New Zealand soldiers acquired this nickname. In the international financial markets, the New Zealand dollar, the basic currency unit, is often called the kiwi, as well. The dollar coin features a kiwi bird on one side.

With all of the other uses of the word kiwi, perhaps the best-known kiwi of all is the tasty and delicious kiwifruit.

This gesture, used to defy one's adversaries, was traditionally seen in battles and now can be seen on the playing field.

Kiwifruit originated in China, and they were grown for decades in New Zealand gardens as Chinese gooseberries. However, when enterprising and industrious New Zealand farmers began propagating the fruit intensively for export, it was given the name kiwifruit, and it is now distributed worldwide.

New Zealand is a peaceful country with little crime and a comfortable lifestyle. The people are friendly and outgoing. One-quarter of the land is protected wilderness and relatively

New Zealand is located about 1,000 miles southeast of Australia in the South Pacific. This mountainous island nation was formed by volcanoes, and is still prone to earthquakes and volcanic eruptions.

free of pollution. New Zealand has its share of distinguished world figures, too. In 1953 New Zealander Sir Edmund Hillary was the first person to climb Mount Everest. A New Zealander invented bungee jumping. And New Zealand has won more Olympic gold medals per capita than any other country.

Ninety Mile Beach is one of the many scenic areas that draws tourists from around the world to New Zealand.

New Zealand's Natural Landscapes

N**ew Zealand consists of North Island and South Island—plus a number of smaller islands. Although these two main islands may look small on the map, they are larger than Great Britain and about the same size as Japan or California. The Cook Strait separates North Island and South Island. North Island is smaller than South Island, but most New Zealanders live there because there is more level land, and temperatures are milder. Stewart Island, located about 20 miles south of South Island, is the third largest island of New Zealand. New Zealand is in the South Pacific directly in the path of the prevailing westerly winds, which are the strong and continuous winds blowing across the ocean from the west. This island nation is located over 1,000 miles southeast of Australia**

Mountains and hills cover almost three-fourths of New Zealand.

On South Island, the spectacular glaciated Southern Alps rise from the Tasman Sea and dominate the island. These mountains have often been described as one of the world's most spectacular mountain ranges. The Southern Alps rise above 5,000 feet (about 1,500 meters), with some glaciated summits over 10,000 feet (about 3,000 meters). They run almost the entire length of the island. On the isolated southwest coast of South Island, these mountains are deeply cut by coastal fjords—long, narrow, glacially scoured, fingerlike extensions of the ocean. Mount Cook (or Aoraki), New Zealand's highest peak rising to 12,283 feet (3,754 meters), is found here in the Southern Alps. The Southern Alps are surrounded by steeply sloping valleys and are crowned with glaciers. The Maoris call them Te Tapu Nui (Peaks of Intense Sacredness). East of the Southern Alps, small areas of coastal plain are found between the cities of Christchurch and Invercargill.

The mountains of North Island are less imposing, but many peaks exceed 5,000 feet (1,500 meters). New Zealand's location on the Pacific Ring of Fire makes the country prone to earthquakes and volcanic eruptions. North Island has four volcanic peaks that are separated by a volcanic plateau. The volcanic plateau contains many hot springs, steam vents called fumaroles, and beautiful geysers. It is a strange environment that seems unearthly and like something from a science-fiction movie set. Ruapehu, Ngauruhoe, and Tongariro are currently active volcanic peaks that threaten to erupt on this island. These peaks rise high over the nearby tablelands, attaining heights of over 9,100 feet (2,775 meters). Most of the rest of North Island is plains and rolling hills.

Other inhabited islands include Stewart Island, the Chatham Islands, and Great Barrier Island. The largest of the uninhabited outlying islands are the Auckland Islands, Campbell Island, the Antipodes Islands, and the Kermadec Islands.

View of Lake Matheson and the Southern Alps. These glaciated mountains run nearly the length of South Island and can provide a challenge to hikers.

Stewart Island is a birdwatchers delight! The kiwi, rare on both North Island and South Island, is common over much of this island. It is especially seen around beach areas. Other birds found on Stewart Island include tuis, parakeets, kakas, and bellbirds. The northern part of the

New Zealand is known for its volcanic activity. This view of one cone was shot from above White Island.

island has a good network of walking paths, but the southern portion is undeveloped and very isolated. The weather is very changeable on this almost uninhabited island.

Great Barrier Island lies at the mouth of the Hauraki Gulf. The island possesses acres of long, white sandy beaches on its eastern shore. The western shore has many deepwater sheltered inlets. A rugged spine of steep ridges runs down the center of Great Barrier Island. There are many natural hot springs and beautiful towering kauri forests on this island. A number of walking trails that combine old logging tracks and tramways guarantee access to most parts of the island.

Climate

New Zealand has a mild marine west-coast climate. The climate here is much like the coastal areas of our Pacific Northwest. Temperatures are mild all year because of the pervading influence of the surrounding oceans and its temperate midlatitude location. New Zealand has four separate and distinct seasons that become more distinct the farther south one travels. Winters are foggy, cloudy, and rainy, but summers are usually warm and sunny. Most of North Island has a subtropical climate. The coastal lowlands near Auckland are mild and wet year-round. However, the area's volcanic peaks create their own micro-climates, with vegetation ranging from fern forests at the base of the mountains to snowcapped peaks at the summits. The warmest area of New Zealand is found on the northern peninsula of North Island. The coolest area is Stewart Island in the distant south.

Since no part of New Zealand lies far from the ocean, temperature extremes are rare. However, it is important to note that maritime climates can change rapidly with severe consequences. Winter falls during June through August, and summer stretches from December through February. The temperature during the warm months usually average 60 to 70 degrees F (16 to 21 degrees C), and during cool months the temperatures average between 40 to 50 degrees F (4 to 10 degrees C). The higher elevations have more severe temperatures, and a few mountain glaciers can be found in high elevations on both islands.

Days start to get noticeably shorter during April, and the first ski resorts open their doors in mid-May. Some ski resorts will stay open until the end of October. The resort towns themselves at the base of the mountains rarely get snow, so it is possible to take the chair lift up the snow-covered mountain, then ski back down to play a game of golf the same day. Visitors to New Zealand usually prefer to come in the summer when it is warm and sunny. However, there are advantages to visiting at other times. In autumn the weather is usually dry and mild, although the evenings may be cool and perhaps even frosty in the south. The frosts help produce spectacular displays of flaming foliage, and there is a plentiful harvest of fruits, especially pears and apples.

New Zealand also lies in the path of the prevailing moisture-bearing westerly winds that bring ample precipitation to the islands. The droughts that plague Australia do not occur here. North Island and South Island have two distinctly different patterns of rainfall based on their differing geological formations. The Southern Alps on South Island act as a barrier for the moisture-laden winds from the Tasman Sea. The westward slopes of the Southern Alps receive a great deal of precipitation each year. Some areas of the west coast receive up to 320 inches (813 centimeters) of rain annually. As the westerlies rise over the Southern Alps, rain and snow fall on the windward side of the range. The windward side is the side of the mountains that faces the wind. Dry air descending the leeward side of the mountain (facing away from the wind), results in some areas receiving only 14 inches (36 centimeters) of rain per year. This "rain shadow" is similar to the dry areas east of the Sierra Nevada, Cascades, and Rocky Mountains in North America. In fact, the Otago region, inland from Dunedin, sits partly in the rain shadow of the Southern Alps. Its rolling, open plains resemble the semiarid expanses of North America's intermountain West. Lowlands usually receive more than 30 inches (76 centimeters) per year in a fairly even distribution. Highlands often receive over 130 inches (330 centimeters).

The North Island has a much more even pattern of rainfall because it lacks the high mountains of South Island. Temperatures are a few degrees cooler on South Island, and both islands receive some snowfall in the winter. The prevailing westerlies are gentle breezes during the summer months but turn into roaring gales during the winter.

Rugged terrain and heavy precipitation in the Southern Alps and in the mountainous center of North Island explain why nearly one-third of New Zealand is uninhabited. Approximately one-fifth of the country is all but useless for any economic purpose beyond tourism. Almost all Maori live on North Island, which also contains the largest city, Auckland, and the national capital, Wellington.

On South Island, most New Zealanders favor the east coast, and the major cities are all located along this coast. The Franz Josef Glacier is a popular geographic feature of South Island. The Maori called this glacier "the tears of the avalanche goddess." The glacier creeps into a rain-forested valley and is cut with several deep crevasses, or fissures, in the glacier's surface. Tourists can sign up for guided hikes over the glacier. Hikers wear boots studded with steel crampons that bite into the ice for a good grip on the icy surface. An ice cave is situated at the base of the Franz Josef Glacier, and a river running out of the ice cave acts as the glacier's plumbing system by flushing glacial runoff. A dozen waterfalls spill over the edges of the glacier and down into the valley.

North of Dunedin, along the Pacific shores of South Island, a group of nearly spherical rocks called the Morioka Rocks lie strewn along the Pacific shores of South Island. These rocks, nearly as tall as a man, were formed four million years ago like pearls. The boulders began from a bit

Three Kings Islands

Whangarai

TASMAN

SEA

Great Barrier
Island

Takapuna
Auckland
Manukau

North
Island   Hamilton

Bay of Plenty

Tauranga

Wakatane

Taupo

L. Taupo

Gisborne

NEW

New Plymouth

Napier   Hawke
Bay
Hastings

Wanganui

Palmerston
North

Collingwood

Cook Strait

Masterton

Nelson

WELLINGTON

Blenheim

Clarence

Greymouth

Waiau

ZEALAND

Waimakariri

Pegasus Bay

Christchurch

Ashburton

Lake
Ellesmere

SOUTH

Timaru

South
Island

PACIFIC

L. Wanaka

Waitaki

Oamaru

OCEAN

L. Wakatipu

Te Anau

Dunedin

Invercargill

Foveaux Strait

Stewart
Island

South Cape

Antipodes Islands

New Zealand is made up of two major islands, each of which is roughly the size
of California. Since South Island is dominated by the Southern Alps, the majority
of residents live on North Island.

of wood, bone, or rock and grew in the sediment of the beach until the wind and sea eroded away the sand. Then they rolled up on the shore.

New Zealand's interesting natural landscapes draw many tourists from around the world and make travel and tourism a source of income for the country.

Kiwis cannot fly, so this road sign reminds all drivers to "brake for kiwi" in those areas where they are likely to be seen.

3

New Zealand's Unique Plant and Animal Life

N
ew Zealand has been separated from other landmasses for more than 100 million years. This has allowed many ancient plants and animals to survive and evolve in isolation. In fact, the evolution of such distinctive species has caused scientists to describe New Zealand as the closest they can get to studying life on another planet. Naturalist David Bellamy has called New Zealand "Moa's Ark" after the native, but now extinct, giant flightless moa bird.

Many of New Zealand's indigenous species are endemic (found only in New Zealand). In contrast, Great Britain, which has been separated from Europe for just 10,000 years, has only one endemic plant and one endemic animal species. Yet approximately 90 percent of New Zealand's insects and marine mollusks; 80 percent of its trees, ferns, and flowering plants; 25 percent of its bird species; all 60 reptiles; 4 species of frogs; and 2 species of bats are found nowhere else on earth.

Flightless Birds

New Zealand has many unique bird species not found in any other part of the world. A grouping of species evolved here that is notable for their large size, flightlessness, and lack of fear of predators. For many of these birds there were no predators to be afraid of since the bat was the only mammal to evolve on the islands of New Zealand. Over millennia, several bird species lost the use of their wings. The largest of 11 species of the moa stood six feet tall. New Zealand's native birds adopted lifestyles and developed in ways unlike that of birds elsewhere. For example, nowhere else in the world is there a bird like the kiwi with its loose hairlike feathers and nostrils at the *end* of its beak.

Unfortunately, today 43 of the 93 native species of birds have become extinct, and 37 species are endangered. The most recent species to go extinct was the huia in 1907. The takahe was believed to be extinct until a few birds were found in the Murchison Mountains in 1948. The rarest bird is the fairy tern, with only 36 remaining in New Zealand. Fairy terns also breed in Australia, but other rare birds, such as the kakapo, takahe, taiko, and black robin among others live and breed nowhere else in the world than New Zealand.

The only flightless parrot on Earth, the kakapo, is found here. This large bird is nocturnal in its habits. With only about 60 kakapos in existence, they are in grave danger of extinction, and efforts are under way to preserve the species. The surviving kakapos have all been transferred to outlying islands in an attempt to keep them out of reach of introduced predatory mammals, such as feral (or wild) cats.

The Kiwi—National Symbol

The best-known bird is the kiwi, New Zealand's unofficial national symbol. Found only in New Zealand, the kiwi is a large wingless bird with hairlike feathers related to the ostrich of Africa, the emu of Australia, and the now-extinct moa of New Zealand. It is about the size of a domestic hen and has an extremely long beak, which it uses to pull worms and insects out of the ground. Females are larger than males, and in some species, such as the brown kiwi, the male is responsible for sitting on the nest and incubating the eggs. Kiwis live in pairs and mate for life, sometimes for as long as 30 years. The kiwi is active only at night, and there are several unique kiwi houses where visitors can watch the kiwis under special nocturnal lighting.

Only about 70,000 kiwis are now left in New Zealand. It is expected that their numbers will continue to drop steadily and perhaps to extinction if the present rate of decline continues. Introduced predators are the biggest threat to kiwi. Stoats, which are a kind of weasel, and cats kill 95 percent of kiwi chicks before they are six months old. Adult kiwis are also attacked and killed by animals. New Zealand's Department of Conservation protects kiwi nests in the wild and raises chicks in captivity to be released when they are old enough to defend themselves from cats and stoats. Ongoing research into their genetics, breeding, and habitat requirements as well as educating the public are other measures being used to help save the kiwi. To both the indigenous Maori and the descendants of the white settlers the kiwi is a *taonga*, or national treasure, and a part of the unique heritage of New Zealand.

The Mischievous Kea

The kea is an especially mischievous bird that loves to approach humans, upset garbage cans, and slide down corrugated roofs at night "kee-aaaing!" This bird is an endemic parrot found mostly in the high country of South Island and is touted as one of the most intelligent birds in the world. The kea is a very inquisitive and nomadic social bird. These characteristics enable the kea to find and make use of new food sources, which they explore with their strong beaks. Keas are a protected species and

Keas can be a pest to campers and hikers who either feed the birds or do not carry out their garbage.

eat a largely vegetarian diet supplemented by occasional grubs and insects. The size of the wild population is unknown, but it is estimated at between 1,000 and 5,000 birds.

Over the past few years, there has been increased human activity in the mountainous areas where keas live. This has brought the kea into frequent contact with humans, and sometimes the contact has resulted in problems. Human garbage and food scraps have become a high-energy food source for the kea, and they have taken to loitering around trash bins and campsites. Campers and well-meaning tourists often feed them scraps or otherwise encourage them to eat human food. This

The tuatara is considered to be a living fossil, having changed very little in 220 million years.

sort of diet is very unhealthy for the kea and discourages the young from looking for the berries, roots, shoots, and insect larvae that make up a normal healthy kea diet. Campers and tourists are asked to forego feeding the birds to discourage them from becoming dependent on an unhealthy food source.

Reptiles

While New Zealand has no snakes at all, it does have a "living fossil." The tuatara, a spiky-backed reptile that resembles lizards, is believed to be the last representative on earth of reptiles that appeared at the same time dinosaurs were evolving, around 220 million years ago. Taturas develop and grow very slowly. Females do not lay their soft-shelled eggs until 9 months after mating, after which the eggs take from 11 to 16 months to hatch. Young tuataras take from 9 to 14 years to reach maturity and attain their full size at 25 to 35 years of age. This reptile has a lifespan of 60 to 100 years. It exists in close proximity to burrowing seabirds such as the petrel and the shearwater. Tuatara share their burrows and feast on the beetles, worms, millipedes, and spiders that make up the bulk of their diet. The tuatara has adapted well to the modern-day conditions in its native New Zealand, living on offshore islands where it numbers approximately 100,000. Well-protected from rats, cats, and pigs, tuataras exist on these islands in their natural habitat and in sanctuaries elsewhere in New Zealand.

Marine Life

New Zealand's offshore waters are home to a variety of fish, including tuna, marlin, snapper, travally, kahawai, and shark, as well as marine mammals: dolphins, whales, and seals. Jellyfish can be found very occasionally along parts of the New Zealand coastline. (Jellyfish stings can be quite painful and are best treated with a splash of vinegar and antihistamines.) Nature lovers from around the world come to observe these creatures. Hector's dolphin, one of the world's rarest dolphins—currently thought to number fewer than 2,500—is unique to New Zealand. Their numbers are declining rapidly because they drown when they entangle in gill nets set out to catch fish. An organization, New Zealand Whale and Dolphin Trust, has aided the Department of Conservation in establishing a Marine Mammal Sanctuary near Banks Peninsula to help protect dwindling populations of Hector's dolphins. Gill-net fishing is now restricted within the sanctuary to reduce the number of these dolphins being killed.

Weta: Flightless Beetles

Weta are the second largest insects in the world, second only to the African goliath beetle. Having lived virtually unchanged for 190 million years, weta have evolved into more than 100 different species, all endemic to New Zealand. These large, flightless beetles are the gentle giants of the insect world: A pregnant female weta on Little Barrier Island weighed in at about 10 pounds (4.5 kilograms). Even the smaller Stephens Island weta is twice the weight of some mice. Wetas look very ferocious and fearsome, especially when they rear up on their spiny back legs. Many of the giant species of weta survive only on protected land, and some are now endangered. In recent years New Zealand's Department of Conservation has established several weta protection programs, which move various species of weta to New Zealand's smaller islands in an effort to establish protected populations and ensure survival of the species.

Pekapeka: New Zealand's Bat

Bats are New Zealand's only indigenous land mammals. An ancient Maori proverb refers to bats as *pekapeka* (the only native mammal of New Zealand) and associates them with the *hokioi*, a night-flying bird that portends death or disaster. New Zealand has two surviving species of bats: long-tailed and lesser short-tailed. The long-tailed bat has a membrane attached to the length of its tail that it uses to scoop up insects as it flies through the air. The long-tailed bat is the more common and is widely distributed throughout the mainland and on some of the larger islands of New Zealand. The short-tailed species of bat has a short, free tail. Unlike most species of bats, the short-tailed bat has adapted to hunting on the ground, using its front limbs to scramble around, and is one of the few species of bats that spends large amounts of time on the forest floor. The lesser short-tailed bat is an endangered species found only on a few scattered sites on the islands of New Zealand. The bat population has declined in New Zealand in recent years because land is being cleared rapidly for farming, and native forests are being logged. As is the case with the kiwi, introduced predators such as rats, stoats, and cats have disturbed bat roosting areas and have contributed to their declining numbers. Both species of bat are fully protected, and a recovery plan to establish new populations is under way.

Plant Life

About 10 to 15 percent of the total land area of New Zealand is covered with native flora, most of which is protected in national reserves and parks. Much of New Zealand's flora is endemic, being found nowhere else in the world. The giant kauri trees, among the largest trees in the world, are now only found in relatively small pockets in Northland and on the Coromandel Peninsula. Even though humans have cleared the land for over 1,000 years, approximately one-fourth of New Zealand—mostly the high country—is still covered in forests. Most of New Zealand's forested areas are covered by temperate rain forests of evergreens, giant tree ferns, vines, and "air plants"—epiphytes—such as orchids. These forested areas are protected in national and forest parks where everyone can enjoy their beauty.

Kauri Tree: Mighty And Vanishing

The kauri tree is one of the world's mightiest trees. They often grow to more than 150 feet (50 meters) tall, with trunk diameters of up to 17 feet (5.2 meters). Kauri covered most of the northern portion of North Island by the time the first humans arrived 1,000 years ago. Maori used the timber to build houses and boats. They also chewed the gum of the kauri tree after soaking it in water and then mixing it with the sap of another plant.

Europeans arrived in New Zealand in the 1800s and began cutting down the mighty kauri forests. Sailors used the straight, polelike trunks of young kauri for ships' masts and spars. Settlers quickly realized the timber from logs of clean, straight, mature kauri trees was superior for building houses. Kauri

These men are dwarfed by the kauri tree they are felling. Europeans found many uses for these, and today all the largest kauri trees are in sanctuaries under government protection.

forests were also exploited mercilessly for the gum, which was often harvested by bleeding live trees. This gum was an essential ingredient used in the manufacture of varnishes. Kauri forests are home to many other trees and plants that live in the diverse understory and shrub layers beneath the kauri canopy.

The largest kauri tree still in existence is called Tane Mahuta. It is 169 feet (51.5 meters) tall and grows in the remote Waipoua Sanctuary of Northland, forests now under the protection of New Zealand's Department of Conservation. The second and third largest kauri trees are also sheltered from danger in the Waipoua Sanctuary.

The Problem of Survival

New Zealand was one of the last places on Earth to be settled by humans. When they eventually arrived about 1,000 years ago, the impact on indigenous species was great. Many of these species became extinct, and close to 1,000 more continue to be threatened by the destruction of habitats, animal pests, and invasive weeds. New Zealand lost several of the larger bird species first, including all 11 species of the giant flightless moa.

By 1600 up to one-third of all forest habitat had been burned and replaced by grasslands. Hunting and loss of habitat made another 23 land-based native bird species go extinct. Once the Europeans arrived and brought their animals during the mid-1800s, New Zealand experienced another drastic reduction in natural habitat. The Europeans converted another one-third of New Zealand's forests into farmlands and extensively drained many wetlands.

Conservation Efforts

New Zealand's plants and animals are unlike any other in the world. The ecosystems and diversity of the species found in them are so unique that without ongoing and vigilant conservation efforts, this diversity will be lost forever to the world.

Realizing the seriousness of this problem, New Zealand has taken impressive measures to protect and enhance the survival of the remaining native species. New Zealand's Department of Conservation administers 30 percent of New Zealand's land area in a series of national parks and protected areas. Thirteen national parks, three maritime parks, and two world-heritage areas have been established. In addition, hundreds of nature reserves and ecological areas are now set aside to preserve the native species. A network of marine reserves and wetlands serves to protect marine species of both plants and animals, and special lakes and rivers are protected under federal law. The Department of Conservation works with special-interest groups and private landowners to ensure the survival of New Zealand's plants and animals and their habitats.

In addition, research and management programs have been started to encourage the recovery of rare and endangered species like the kakapo, kiwi, and tuatara. How successful are New Zealand's conservation efforts? Attitudes toward preserving the natural environment have improved over the past two decades, and active conservation efforts have been greatly strengthened. There have been breakthroughs in threatened species management, including better pest control, extending protected areas on land and sea, and restoring offshore island sanctuaries, all of which have had a great impact. In fact, the decline of some species has actually been stopped.

Revegetation projects are slowly restoring native habitat to New Zealand's islands. Several island sanctuaries are now free of all introduced predators, and many endangered birds and reptiles have been moved to safer locations like Tiritiri Matangi and Little Barrier Island. Mainland sanctuaries are also monitored closely so that native species may thrive safely. The goal is to conserve the natural habitats and ecosystems that still exist. New Zealand has shown itself to be a world leader in bringing species back from the brink of extinction. With continued efforts, its great and unique biodiversity will continue to thrive and fascinate the world.

Engraving of a Maori chief with characteristic facial tattoos.

4

New Zealand Through Time

The first people to reach New Zealand were the Moa hunters, who arrived about 1,000 years ago. Named after the huge, flightless birds they hunted for food, these people fished and hunted and were probably of East Polynesian ancestry

The Polynesian navigator Kupe has been credited with the discovery of New Zealand in 950 A.D. He named it Aotearoa—the Land of the Long White Cloud. (Most travelers to New Zealand notice this long white cloud, too. This mass of moisture is caused by the powerful westerly winds and ocean currents that speed around the Southern Hemisphere unimpeded by landmasses.) Centuries later, around 1350 A.D., a great migration of people from Kupe's homeland, Hawaiki in Polynesia, followed his directions and sailed to New

Zealand. These people arrived in seven canoes and were called Maoris. According to Maori oral history, they eventually replaced or blended in with the Moa people who were already there.

The first European to set foot in New Zealand was a Dutch explorer, Abel Tasman, in 1642. (During this same voyage he discovered the island that was eventually named Tasmania in his honor.) He was searching for the legendary great southern continent. He sailed along the western coast of New Zealand first. When he tried to land, several of his crewmen were killed by the Maoris; however, he succeeded in sketching sections of the two main islands' west coasts. In 1769, during one of his three South Pacific voyages, Captain James Cook and sailed around the two main islands in his ship, the *Endeavor*. Captain Cook's first contacts with the Maoris also proved violent, but he persisted and eventually was able to claim the land for the British crown before setting sail for Australia.

The Treaty of Waitangi

When the British first colonized New Zealand in the 1840s, they treated it as a branch of the Australian venture in whaling and sealing. From 1839 to 1841 New Zealand was under the jurisdiction of New South Wales, a state of Australia. The increasing numbers of British settlers who came to New Zealand caused a few problems, however. Lumbering, whaling, and seal hunting attracted them to New Zealand, but they and the Maoris continually fought over land. Knowing that something had to be done, the representatives of the British Crown and the leading Maori chiefs signed a treaty in 1840. This treaty was called the Treaty of Waitangi because it was signed at Waitangi in the Bay of Islands—now one of New Zealand's most historic sites. The signing of the Treaty of Waitangi began on February 6, which has become New Zealand's national

Captain James Cook (1728–1779) received a typically unfriendly reception by the Maori when he visited New Zealand in 1769, but despite this he laid claim to the country for the glory of England.

day: Waitangi Day. The Treaty of Waitangi established the country as a nation and gave the British sovereignty over New Zealand. The Maoris, in return, retained possession of their land and were promised the protection of the British government.

The Waitangi Treaty House is a powerful symbol to both the Maori and the descendants of the British settlers. In 1995 during a planned celebration, some Maori activists tried to burn down the small house to protest the perceived bad faith shown by white New Zealanders in honoring that treaty.

Relations between the British and the Maoris soon deteriorated because the British ignored the treaty rights given to the Maoris. When the Maori signed the treaty for British "guns, goods, and money," they thought they were granting the British the right to use the land in exchange for a trading relationship. The Maori did not regard land as a tradable commodity, but rather as an asset of the people as a whole. To them, their land was sacred and full of spiritual significance. However, the British felt the treaty gave them *exclusive* rights to Maori lands on which to settle British colonists. The British also thought the treaty gave them the right to extract wealth from the land through farming, mining, and forestry. In 1860 war broke out between the two groups. This fighting went on for almost a decade before the British and colonial forces finally defeated the determined Maori, many of whom died from disease and warfare during this period.

In the 50 years following the signing of the treaty, the Maori went from occupying all of New Zealand to occupying just 16 percent of the land. Meanwhile the British occupied the rest of New Zealand. The Maori gradually recovered from population decline and began to intermarry with settlers and missionaries. They adopted much of the European culture, too. In recent decades, Maori have become increasingly urbanized and more politically active and culturally assertive.

Constitutional Government

Constitutional government began to develop in the 1850s. In 1867 the Maori won the right to a certain number of reserved seats in Parliament. During this period the livestock industry began to expand, and New Zealand started to acquire the characteristics of a modern economy. By the 1890s parliamentary government was well established along the lines of a democracy.

New Zealand was declared a dominion by royal proclamation in 1907. It achieved full internal and external autonomy by the Statute of Westminster Adoption Act of 1947. This merely formalized a situation that had existed for many years.

Continuing Ethnic Unrest

Finally in 1985, after many years of unrest, New Zealand's government overhauled the Treaty of Waitangi and gave financial reparations to several Maori tribes whose land had been wrongfully confiscated. Additionally, the government of New Zealand has made several recent attempts to mend relations with the Maori groups. However, these were poorly conceived and administered reparation programs that have only outraged many Maoris. There has been much ill will and an upsurge of militant Maori protests.

Violence erupted on Waitangi Day in 1995 at the annual ceremony honoring the treaty signing. The prime minister, other officials, and several visitors were gathered at the old wooden treaty house where the original treaty of Waitangi had been signed. They were celebrating the highlight of the day's events when Maori burst in and disrupted the ceremonies. The Maori tried to burn the old wooden treaty house down, and the panicking crowd jostled the prime minister. For the first time in more than half a century, the ceremony had to be abandoned.

Like the Australian aborigines, the Maoris have filed claims against the government of New Zealand to recover their traditional tribal lands. Maori leaders insist that the terms of the Waitangi Treaty be enforced. This would mean that large tracts in both urban and rural areas—over half the land in New Zealand—would revert to Maori ownership. The government has made several concessions, including giving the Maoris the legal right to fish in offshore waters without a fishing license.

Maoris have disrupted events, set up roadblocks, occupied land-claim areas, and threatened to blow up the New Zealand parliament building. The violence and unrest shocked New Zealanders. Attempts to appease the Maori and make amends for past wrongs are topics at the top of the national agenda. Race relations are more stable once again, but the issue remains vitally important.

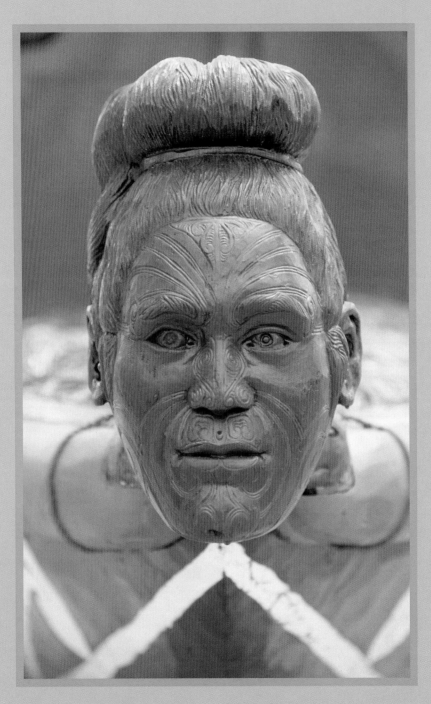

A beautiful wood carving on the prow of a Maori war canoe.

5

People and Culture

Most of the four million New Zealanders are of British origin. They are commonly called the *Paheka*, which is Maori for "white people." British colonization guaranteed the dominance of their cultural traditions by the late 19th century. In addition to the white majority, approximately 10 percent of New Zealanders claim descent from the indigenous Maori population, who are of Polynesian origin. English and Maori are the official languages of New Zealand. English is more widely spoken although recently the Maori language is making a comeback. Maori is a musical, poetic language that is easy to pronounce.

The Maori seemed destined for extinction in the early 1900s; however, their numbers have rebounded significantly. The Maori are most numerous on North Island, with a sizeable community living in the city of Auckland. Although the Maoris' socioeconomic standing is still depressed, they are much better off than Australian aborigines. While the Maoris are blending in with the white population socially and racially, there is an active Maori political movement that resists change. This Maori cultural and political movement resists the loss of traditional culture that may occur with ongoing integration

Ethnic minorities of East Indians and Chinese also live on the islands of New Zealand. Asians now make up 5 percent of New Zealand's population and are responsible for many contributions to New Zealand's culture and economy. There are also approximately 167,000 Pacific Islanders living in New Zealand. Auckland has the largest Polynesian population of any city in the world. During the late 1870s, natural increase replaced immigration as the main reason for population growth. The increased birth rate in New Zealand has accounted for more than 75 percent of its population growth in the 20th century.

In the late 1990s some 30,000 to 50,000 immigrants per year were approved to become citizens of New Zealand. People from Europe made up the largest regional group of migrants, followed by East Asian countries.

While New Zealand has a strong British heritage, the culture has matured into a unique and distinct culture during the 20th century. Increasing 20th century globalization helped New Zealand forge an independent identity. Because of television and movies, New Zealand is now more closely linked with Australia, continental Europe, and the United States. For example, the most famous movie ever produced in New Zealand is *The Lord of the Rings,* filmed by the country's most acclaimed director, Peter Jackson. For many viewers this was their introduction to the spectacular beauty for which New Zealand is known.

Cities of New Zealand

New Zealand, like Australia, is a highly Westernized, very urbanized nation. Therefore, almost 85 percent of New

The Sky Tower in the city of Auckland is the highest structure in the Southern Hemisphere.

Zealand's population live in urban areas, where the service and manufacturing industries are growing rapidly. Almost 75 percent of the people, including a large majority of Maori, live on North Island. Only six urban areas have an estimated population of more than 100,000.

Auckland is the largest city in New Zealand with approximately 1.2 million people in the metropolitan area. Sky Tower, the tallest structure in the Southern Hemisphere at 1,076 feet (328 meters), shines its lights down on the surrounding city at night. Forty volcanic vents and seven extinct volcanoes encircle Auckland. The most prominent volcanic slope is Eden's Hill, where the remains of a Maori fortress cover the summit. The Auckland Museum houses an extensive collection of Maori and Polynesian artifacts, including a war canoe measuring 80 feet (24 meters) long.

The capital city, Wellington, has a metropolitan area population of 365,000 and is situated on a splendid harbor on the southern tip of North Island. However, the weather can be quite nasty in Wellington, with winds of gale force in the wintertime. Nonetheless, this lively city of culture and the arts—boasting monthly festivals—is the center of government for New Zealand and is home to many of the country's national treasures.

The other four urban centers are: Napier-Hastings (population 120,000), Hamilton (population 150,000), Christchurch (population 358,000), and Dunedin (population 114,000). Approximately one-half of New Zealand's population lives in these six small cities. All of these cities have English names currently, but there is a movement underway to replace them with the original Maori place-names.

All of the major cities in New Zealand are centered on vibrant downtown areas similar to those of North American cities. Since all of New Zealand's major cities are on the coast, waterfront districts and port settings give them interesting harbor settings. These cities are noted for their low crime rates, lack of slums, and relatively clean streets. Efficient

The ornate wood carving on many of the Maori war canoes has earned them a place in some of New Zealand's finest museums.

transportation systems and expanding suburbs cause these cities to resemble North American urban spaces.

Just as in Anglo America, upscale neighborhoods with all the amenities, retirement communities, and pricey suburbs continually draw more people. This creates pressure on the cities' services as urban areas struggle to provide these new inhabitants with water, waste disposal, streets,

The capital city of Wellington and Wellington Harbor are situated at the base of the Tinakori Hills on North Island.

hospitals, fire and police protection, and all the other necessary public services.

Settlement on South Island is clustered in the drier lowlands and coastal districts east of the mountains. Christchurch is the largest urban center on South Island. It straddles the two-mile-high Southern Alps and the Pacific Ocean. It is situated on the Canterbury Plains, where the largest concentration of cultivated land in New Zealand is found. Christchurch is a convenient base for many expeditions to the South Pole. It is also the staging area for bringing in supplies to the United States's three permanent bases in Antarctica and New Zealand's own base for scientific research. Antarctic Centre, a museum devoted to Antarctica, is a popular attraction for visitors to Christchurch, containing a room designed to simulate the conditions found on Antarctica—the coldest, driest place on earth.

The rest of New Zealand is sparsely populated due to the rugged, mountainous terrain.

Rural New Zealand

Large areas of rural settlement are spread throughout New Zealand. New Zealand's rural landscape includes many agricultural activities, though most of the agricultural land is devoted to livestock grazing. Commercial livestock outnumber people by a ratio of almost 15 to 1, so it is not surprising to see sheep and cattle grazing everywhere. Sheep graze on imported European grasses from the remote pastures of South Island to the volcanic slopes of North Island. Dairy operations also proliferate, especially in the humid lowlands of the north near Auckland. One of the most fertile zones of specialized farming is centered on the Canterbury Plains near Christchurch. British colonizer Edward Gibbon Wakefield chose this productive ground for English settlement, and the Canterbury Plains now abound with fruit orchards, grain fields, and vegetable gardens.

Education and Literacy

New Zealand's population is highly literate, with 99 percent of citizens aged 15 and older able to read and write. However, as is the case for many other indigenous peoples

In a land where livestock outnumber people by 15 to 1, sheep ranches are a common sight in the countryside.

around the world, Maori schooling is irregular, and their levels of advanced education are far below average in New Zealand. The educational system is distinctly British, and the schools of New Zealand are full of British traditions. Teachers and administrators enjoy morning tea at 10 A.M., and for 15 to 30 minutes they chat and share news over their tea and coffee while students entertain themselves nearby. School uniforms are another British tradition that New Zealanders embrace. Many believe that uniforms encourage students to take their education seriously. Students generally wear the school uniform proudly and try to avoid behavior that might disgrace the uniforms. Because of the ethnic diversity of New Zealand's population, school students may be greeted each morning in several languages: *"Kia ora"* in Maori, *"Namaste"* in Hindi, *"Talofa"* in Samoan, or "Good morning" in English.

Many excellent schools and universities offer comprehensive training opportunities, and 80 to 90 percent of secondary-school-aged males and females remain enrolled in school.

Religion

Sixty-seven percent of New Zealand's population is Christian. Because of its British roots, New Zealand's main Protestant denomination is Anglican, but there are also Presbyterian, Baptist, and Methodist churches. Approximately 15 percent of the population is Roman Catholic. While some Maori have converted to Christianity, most follow their traditional animist religion. Traditional Maori animist religion is closely linked with the natural environment. Maoris believe that each component of the natural world, including people, possesses a harmonious life force called *mauri*. People must respect this life force wherever it manifests—in a mountain, a river, or a tree. The Maori realize that humans cannot live on earth without changing it and transforming it, but they feel we must try to damage it as little as possible. Their perspective on the environment often conflicts with the modern development that is rapidly occurring in New Zealand. For example, a Maori recently protested the discharge of sewage into a river, saying that it ruined the river's *mauri*.

Maori artwork reflects their views on the environment, as well. Woodcarvers insist on carving from a piece of natural wood because it retains its *mauri* better than a milled board— thus the finished carving will still contain the forest's *mauri*.

They feel Europeans are careless with the forest's *mauri* when they fell trees and send them to the sawmill.

Art and Theater

The art of New Zealand reflects the values of innovation, integrity, and craftsmanship. It reflects the *Paheka*, Maori, and Melanesian heritage of New Zealanders. Wood, stone, shell, and bone carvings are readily available, while larger works such as *tukutuku* (wood paneling) can be seen in most *maraes* (meetinghouses). *Paua* shell, greenstone, greywacke, and greenwacke pebbles are often fashioned into jewelry that takes inspiration from the verdant landscapes of New Zealand. New Zealand has a significant number of art galleries, including the Dunedin Public Art gallery, which is the oldest viewing room in New Zealand and one of its best. New Zealand also has a lively theater scene, especially in Wellington, and the music scene is vigorous and has given New Zealand a great pool of talent to entertain listeners both locally and overseas.

Social Issues

From its beginnings, New Zealand has been at the forefront of instituting social-equality and social-welfare legislation. As for the former, New Zealand was the first country in the world to accord women the right to vote, in 1893. Approximately one-third of parliamentary seats are held by women. One-third of New Zealand's administrators and managers and almost one-half of all professional and technical workers are women. Women have a good position in New Zealand and participate fully in the work force as well as hold many political offices.

Regarding social-welfare programs, New Zealand has introduced many. The country adopted pensions for the elderly in 1898 and social security for the aged, widows, and orphans in 1938. A child-welfare program was put into practice in 1907 to provide for the care of children and babies. Setting a minimum wage and a 40-hour workweek were positive changes that benefited many workers. Workers are able to collect unemployment checks when they are out of work, and the majority enjoy the benefits of health insurance. New Zealand's system of social services provides high-quality health care to its people. Socialized medicine became the norm in 1938, with medical attention and treatment available to all at a modest cost. Just as in North America and Europe, heart disease and cancer are the leading causes of death. Alcoholism is also a serious problem. The lifespan of New Zealanders averages nearly 79 years, and the rate of child mortality has fallen substantially since 1960.

During a visit to New Zealand in 1995, Queen Elizabeth II donned a traditional Maori cloak and admired Maori woodwork when she visited Rotorua, the center of Maori culture.

6

Government and Politics

N ew Zealand is a modern country with a well-developed economy and a government structure based on the British parliamentary system. New Zealand has been largely self-governing since 1907 and fully independent since 1947. Nonetheless, New Zealand maintains close ties with Great Britain, the nation that claimed the beautiful islands in 1840. It is a fully independent member of the British Commonwealth and has no written constitution of its own.

Great Britain's current reigning monarch, Queen Elizabeth II, is New Zealand's chief of state and is represented by a governor general selected by the monarch. A cabinet led by the prime minister holds executive authority. The prime minister is the leader of the political party or coalition of parties holding the majority of seats in Parliament. The prime minister governs for a three-year term. All cabinet members must be members of Parliament. Parliament has 12 seats, 5 of which are reserved for the Maori, who are elected on a separate Maori ticket. However, Maori may also run for and be elected to nonreserved seats. (This has happened in past elections.) Parliaments are elected for a maximum term of three years, although elections can be called sooner.

The judiciary is composed of the Court of Appeals, the High Court, and the District Courts. New Zealand law has three main sources: English common law, a variety of statutes of the United Kingdom that Parliament enacted before 1947, and statutes of the New Zealand Parliament. The courts are very concerned when interpreting common law and strive to do so in such a manner that it conforms to the way it is interpreted in the United Kingdom. It is very important to preserve the uniformity of legal interpretation. To ensure such uniformity, London maintains a Privy Council that serves as the final court of appeal. Also, judges in New Zealand have made it their practice to follow decisions of British judges, although they are not bound by those decisions.

Local Government

New Zealand is made up of 93 counties, 9 districts, and 3 town districts. Local government in New Zealand has only the powers given to it by Parliament. New Zealand's 13 regional councils are directly elected by the vote of the people. Each regional council has a chairman elected by its members. The responsibilities of the regional councils include regional aspects of civil defense, transportation planning, and environmental management and planning. These regional authorities are directly elected by popular vote. They are permitted to set local tax rates and are responsible for collecting these taxes. Mayors who are also elected by the people head these regional authorities.

The territorial authorities may delegate powers to local community boards. These boards serve the local interests by advocating community concerns and viewpoints. However, community boards have no power or authority to levy taxes, appoint staff, or own property.

Politics in New Zealand

Two political parties dominate New Zealand's political life: the left-leaning Labour Party, which first came into power in 1935, and the conservative National Party.

The National Party won control of the government in 1949 and adopted many welfare measures first begun by the Labour Party. They held power until 1984, with the exception of two brief periods of Labour governments from 1957 to 1960 and 1972 to 1975.

After the Labour government regained control in 1984, it implemented many social and economic policies that included such measures as a comprehensive social-security system and a large-scale public-works policy. It instituted a 40-hour workweek, set a minimum wage, and made union membership mandatory. It also began a series of market-oriented reforms in response to New Zealand's mounting external debt.

The National Party was elected again in October 1990. It was a landslide victory for the party, capturing 67 of 97 parliamentary seats. Some supporters were very disappointed when the National Party continued on with the reforms first begun by the Labour Party. The National Party won the next election by a narrow margin in November 1993. During a referendum, or public vote, at the same time, New Zealanders changed their electoral system to a form of proportional representation similar to Germany's system. This change in electoral system was designed to give smaller parties a greater voice in Parliament. The 1996 election was the first one held under this new "mixed-member-proportional" (MMP) system. The Labor Party was returned to power in 1999, under the leadership of Prime Minister Helen Clark.

Foreign Policy

New Zealanders learned a valuable lesson during World War II when they saw how rapidly the Japanese were able to take over the Malay Peninsula and seize many of the Pacific islands, with Australia likely to be next. They realized that they needed to take some responsibility for safeguarding their own security rather than relying on Great Britain. In 1947, for the first time in the nation's history, New Zealand sought to join regional organizations and groups and work with their neighbors in the Pacific toward common goals. One such organization was the South Pacific Commission. The commission was a regional body that worked to promote the welfare of the Pacific region. This commission grew to include many subassociations that dealt with trade, education, and migration as well as cultural and economic development. New Zealand has served as a leader of this organization in past years. In 1971 it also joined the other independent and self-governing states of the South Pacific to establish the South Pacific Forum. This group meets annually to discuss issues of interest in the region.

New Zealand's current foreign policy is oriented toward developed democratic nations and emerging Pacific Rim economies. The country's major political parties have generally agreed on the broad outlines of foreign policy. The current coalition government has been very active in multilateral forums on issues of ongoing interest and involvement to New Zealand. Some of these issues are of deepest concern to New Zealand are disarmament, arms control, and trade liberalization.

New Zealand is a member of the United Nations and greatly values its participation in that organization. The country is also a contributing member of the World Trade

Organization (WTO), the World Bank, the International Monetary Fund (IMF), the Organization for Economic Cooperation and Development (OECD), the Asia Pacific Economic Cooperation (APEC), the South Pacific Forum, and the International Whaling Commission, among many others. In the past, New Zealand's geographic isolation and its agricultural economy's general prosperity tended to minimize public interest in world affairs. However, growing global trade and other international economic events have made New Zealanders increasingly aware of their country's dependence on stable overseas markets. New Zealand's economic involvement with Asia has been increasingly important. Originally New Zealand gave financial foreign aid to Asian nations, mainly to Southeast Asia. Expanding trade with the growing economies of Asia helped to link New Zealand economically with the other nations of the Pacific Rim.

Relations with the United States

New Zealand has excellent relations with the United States. The countries share common elements of history and culture and a commitment to democratic principles. Senior-level officials regularly consult with each other on issues of mutual interest.

The United States established consular representation in New Zealand in 1839 to represent and protect American shipping and whaling interests. Since the United Kingdom was responsible for New Zealand's foreign affairs, direct diplomatic ties between the two countries were not established until 1942. At that time the Japanese threat encouraged closer cooperation between the United States and New Zealand. During World War II over 400,000 American military personnel were stationed on New Zealand as a staging area for crucial battles such as Guadalcanal and Tarawa.

After World War II, access to New Zealand's port by U.S.

From whale hunting to whale watching, the lives of New Zealanders have been intimately bound up with the sperm whale and other marine mammals. This old engraving shows how close harpooning brought the hunter to his prey.

vessels contributed greatly to the effectiveness and flexibility of U.S. naval forces in the Pacific. In recent years concerns about nuclear testing in the South Pacific led the Labour government to ban nuclear-armed and nuclear-powered warships from New Zealand's harbors. In 1985 a U.S.

destroyer was not allowed to dock at a New Zealand port even though its presence there was for joint ANZUS military maneuvers. (ANZUS is a security alliance of Australia, New Zealand, and the United States, which was reached in 1951.) The crew of the U.S. ship refused to say if there were nuclear weapons on board. They were denied permission to dock, and as a result, in 1986 New Zealand formally withdrew from the ANZUS Alliance.

The standoff regarding nuclear weapons could not be resolved through diplomatic channels, but despite this the government continues to be committed to close economic, political, and social ties with the United States. Much of New Zealand's military maneuvers are now done with Australia.

National Defense and Security

New Zealand has three defense policy objectives: to be able to defend the country against low-level threats from other nations, to contribute to regional security, and to play a part in global security efforts. They are dedicated peacekeepers and wish to keep the peace on a global scale.

National defense needs are not a big concern, but significant upgrades in New Zealand's defense equipment in their defense budget have been made for the next several years. Part of the reason for the country's increased defense spending is the criticism directed against it by other nations that their defense forces have fallen below an acceptable standard. New Zealand sets its own defense standard. It aims to maintain a "credible minimum force" to reassure its neighbors and allies of its commitment to regional stability. New Zealand claims an area of direct strategic concern that extends from Australia to Southeast Asia to the South Pacific. The country's defense expenditures total approximately one percent of its gross domestic product. This minimal contribution that New Zealand sets for itself demands that its foreign allies pick up a much larger share of the tab than they necessarily should. This has been a source of tension to otherwise very favorable and friendly relations with its allies.

Multilateral Peacekeeping Activities

New Zealand plays a very active role in multilateral peacekeeping efforts in the world. It has taken a leading role in trying to bring peace, reconciliation, and reconstruction to Bougainville, an island of Papua New Guinea. New Zealand maintains a contingent in the Sinai Multinational Force and Observers and has contributed to U.N. peacekeeping operations in Angola, Cambodia, Somalia, and the former Yugoslavia. It has also participated in the peacekeeping efforts in the Persian Gulf. In late 2004, New Zealand withdrew its small number of troops from Iraq.

New Zealand participates in Mutual Assistance Programs (MAP), sharing training facilities and exchanges of personnel, and conducting joint exercises with the Philippines, Thailand, Indonesia, Papua New Guinea, Malaysia, Brunei, Singapore, Fiji, Tonga, and other South Pacific states. In addition to its MAP partners, New Zealand conducts military exercises with its Five Power Defense Arrangement partners (Australia, the United Kingdom, Malaysia, and Singapore) as well as with Korea.

Nuclear Testing Issues

A key concern of many of the smaller nations in the Pacific is the issue of nuclear testing. Both the United States and France have tested nuclear devices by exploding them on tiny Pacific atolls. The United States discontinued these tests during the 1960s, but France continued them. Finally a strong desire to end such testing resulted in making the entire Pacific Ocean area a nuclear-free zone. Testing of nuclear devices is totally banned, and even transport of nuclear weapons through the area was prohibited, as was discussed above.

Underwater nuclear testing as well as aboveground tests have been a source of friction between the smaller nations in the Pacific Ocean and the major powers. While the United States has discontinued such tests, the French continued nuclear testing into the 1990s.

New Zealand is still very concerned with the testing of nuclear weapons in the Pacific by the superpowers. The nuclear test ban treaty signed in 1963 limited the United States's role in testing, but France has continued to conduct underground tests. Japan and the United States have explored using remote Pacific atolls for disposal of nuclear waste. When France detonated a nuclear device in French Polynesia in 1995, New Zealand recalled its ambassador from Paris in protest.

There are eleven times as many sheep in New Zealand as there are people and raising sheep has been a mainstay of the economy for two hundred years.

7

The Economy

N ew Zealand's economy is largely based on its exports, and for this reason its fortunes are very much affected by the world economy it serves. The country's industries include tourism, processed foods, minerals, and wood and paper products. New Zealand also produces steel, aluminum, boats, and clothing. Most manufactured goods, however, must be imported.

New Zealand enjoys a high level of prosperity based on exports from its efficient agricultural system. For 200 years the backbone of New Zealand's economy has been raising cattle and sheep. New Zealand is a major exporter of lamb, beef, butter, cheese, and wool—sheep wool remains a major export mainly for the British carpet industry. Interestingly enough, worldwide concerns about the dangers of excess cholesterol in

New Zealander leading a cow to market at the Agricultural Fair.

the diet led not only to the development of sheep with less body fat, but also to a new industry of deer farming—which in turn solved another problem. Introduced from Great Britain as a source of game, deer became a pest that caused overgrazed grasslands, soil erosion, and accelerated the extinction of some native herbivores; however, new consumer tastes solved this problem by providing a market for deer meat. Deer meat, or venison, is low in fat and increasingly in demand by Australia and Europe. Other deer products such as hides and antlers are also in demand in global markets.

Agriculture in New Zealand

Economic development progressed very rapidly on South Island after gold was discovered on the west coast in the 1860s. The gold strike brought many immigrants to New Zealand to seek their fortunes. But most importantly, gold attracted investment money that was used to build roads and railroads. The new transportation network opened up the Canterbury Plain—the best wheat-farming land in New Zealand—to cultivation. The Canterbury Plain has fertile soil, plentiful rain, and a long growing season, all of which support lush pastures for grazing sheep and cattle and rich farmlands for growing fruits, vegetables, and grains. Pioneer settlers grazed sheep beyond the plains in New Zealand's interior mountain region.

New Zealand's mild climate allows a great variety of crops, including grains, vegetables, and fruits. Only 5 percent of New Zealand's land is cultivated, and the main crop is hay and other animal fodder. Still, the nation grows enough food to supply most of its own needs as well as provide for export crops—the leading ones being apples and, New Zealand's best-known fruit, kiwifruit. Although other countries now grow kiwifruits, New Zealand remains the foremost producer in the Southern Hemisphere and is a leader in improving varieties. New Zealand also grows selected grapes for its wine industry. Modern technology and suitable growing techniques

The new industry of deer farming has opened other potential markets for New Zealand.

combine with the right selections of grape varieties to produce high-quality grapes and wines.

Before the formation of the European Union, New Zealand's exporting was largely dependent on British markets. Most of New Zealand's exports to Great Britain were agricultural products such as wool and butter. As recently as the early 1970s, the United Kingdom accounted for roughly 30 percent of New Zealand's trade. When the United Kingdom joined the European Common Market in the 1970s, things changed because of the stringent agricultural protection policies the organization embraced. The Common Market (now the European Union) included countries with surpluses competitive with New Zealand's. Because of this, New Zealand tried to develop its industrial sector and expand trade with other partners such as countries in Asia. New Zealand is developing new markets in many countries. Lamb is a popular export to Muslim countries, and Japan's growing taste for Western foods has given New Zealand a new and thriving market for dairy products and fruits.

A Period of Reform

Unlike Australia, New Zealand does not have a rich base of mineral resources to export to global markets. The economy suffered during the 1970s and 1980s, and the country slipped downward in the ranks of the world's affluent countries. By the 1980s New Zealand had entered a serious recession. This was the first time New Zealanders suffered a decline in their standard of living, and a sizeable number of them emigrated to Australia during this period. They complained about the economic troubles in New Zealand; they also complained of the boredom of living in an isolated country far from the global mainstream.

The recession forced the government of New Zealand to take drastic action, and it enacted stringent social and

Farmers put up elaborate nets over their grape vines to protect the fruit from wild birds.

economic reforms. Since 1984 government subsidies have been eliminated. Also, import regulations have been liberalized, and exchange rates have been freely floated. Controls on interest rates, wages, and prices have also been removed, and marginal rates of taxation have been reduced. Inflation has been cut from an annual rate of more than 18 percent in 1987 to an estimated 2.5 percent in 2004. Tight monetary policy and substantial efforts to reduce the government budget deficit engineered this reduction in inflation. Government-owned enterprises have been restructured and sold to private concerns. This has reduced the government's role in New Zealand's economy and allowed some of the public debt to be retired.

New Zealand had always been a country noted for its high tax rates, hefty social welfare programs, and state ownership of large economic concerns. Now the government was anxious to privatize and sell government-owned enterprises to private individuals and firms. Most state industries were sold off to private parties. Because of this privatization, New Zealand has become one of the most market-oriented countries of the world. A problem arose, however, when these reforms led to an unemployment rate that reached 11 percent in 1991. An improving economy has brought unemployment down to about 4.5 percent by late 2004.

Economic growth reached an unsustainable peak of over 6 percent in 1994 and has since slowed a great deal in response to tighter monetary policy. At the same time, by 2004, real gross-domestic-product growth was increasing at an estimated 3.8 percent annual rate.

Trade Relations With Other Countries

New Zealand's exports were harmed by the rapid appreciation of the New Zealand dollar from late 1994 to mid-1997 that resulted from the tight monetary policy. Monetary policy loosened in 1997, causing the New Zealand currency to lose all of its gains against the U.S. dollar. This led to an increase in exports during the second half of 1997. However, the Asian financial crisis took its toll on such crucial foreign exchange earners as Asian tourism, forestry exports, and educational services. Dairy and meat exports to Asia also suffered in the late 1990s, but manufactured products held up well in the markets. New Zealand commodity exporters have looked to Europe and the United States to replace Asian customers lost during the Asian financial crisis.

Improved relations with Australia have also helped the export picture. New Zealand and Australia adopted a free-trade pact in 1982 called the Closer Economic Relations Agreement (CER), which eliminated almost all trade barriers between the two countries in farm and industrial goods and services. New Zealand benefited because the agreement opened larger Australian markets to New Zealand exports. The agreement also gave Australian banks and corporations better access to business opportunities in New Zealand. Since 1990 CER has created a single market of more than 20 million people, and this has provided new opportunities for New Zealand exporters. Australia is now the destination of about 22 percent of New Zealand's exports, compared to 14 percent in 1983.

The goods and services exported from the United States are increasingly competitive in New Zealand. The market-based economy offers many opportunities for U.S. exporters and importers, and investment opportunities exist in chemicals, food preparation, finance, tourism, forest products, and franchising. The best sales prospects are for software, computers, chemicals, medical equipment, sporting goods, telecommunications, and transportation equipment.

New Zealand is open to foreign investment and encourages it without discrimination. Overseas investment of sums exceeding $6.4 million or investments in commercial fishing and rural land require special approval. This approval comes from New Zealand's Overseas Investment Commission (OIC). Foreign investment in commercial fishing is limited to a 25 percent holding, unless the Ministry of Agriculture

New Zealand's magnificent forests produce lumber that has increasing importance in its economy. Port Chalmers is a major port for lumber leaving the country.

and Fisheries grants a special exemption. The level of foreign ownership is not restricted for rural land. However, foreign purchasers are required to demonstrate that the purchase is beneficial to New Zealand. In practice, approval requirements set by the Overseas Investment Commission have not been an obstacle for U.S. investors. No performance requirements are attached to foreign direct investment, and full remittance of profits and capital is permitted through normal banking channels.

Several U.S. companies have subsidiary branches in New Zealand. Many companies operate through local agents, and some are joint ventures. The U.S. government recognized the generally liberal trading environment in New Zealand by signing a bilateral Trade and Investment Framework Agreement in 1992 that provided for periodic government-to-government consultations on trade and investment issues and concerns.

Current State of the Economy

New Zealand's economic growth rate has somewhat improved over the past two decades. The 2004 estimated annual growth rate stands at 3.8 percent. Meanwhile, the unemployment rate has dropped to about 4.5 percent as of 2004. Nonetheless its per capita income is lower than that of Hong Kong, Japan, and Australia. In 2000 the Labour Party prime minister, Helen Clark, had to cancel a large purchase of F-16 fighter jets from the United States, stating that New Zealand could not afford this purchase. However, there are some positive signs that the country's economic recovery will continue. Inflation hit its lowest rate since the 1930s in 1999 (1.3 percent). Interest rates were also cut, and the government enjoyed a budget surplus.

New Zealand has a moderately high standard of living based on the income derived from the country's 45 million sheep and 10 million cattle. Its per capita Gross National Income in 2004 was approximately $15,900, comparable to that of Israel.

Lush, green pastures cover half the country. Unfortunately, the highly mechanized cattle and sheep industries do not require very many workers. Competition in the dairy industry is intense, and profits are small. Therefore, most New Zealanders work in service jobs and processing industries in New Zealand's three largest cities: Auckland, Christchurch, and Wellington.

New Zealand, like Australia, is trying to diversify its economy so that the country will not be so dependent on raising sheep and cattle. It is difficult to do, however, because New Zealand does not have the mineral resources needed for industry. The country must import oil, though it has large quantities of coal and offshore natural-gas deposits, and hydroelectric power and geothermal energy supply more than 80 percent of the country's electricity. While New Zealand is not rich in natural resources, the country does have some iron and gold deposits, and its magnificent natural forests produce exports that have become increasingly important as the country tries to reduce its dependency on sheep and dairy exports.

Diversification of industry is difficult due to several factors. New Zealand is far from many world markets. Local industries are built on a small scale, and the local market for goods is limited. High labor costs also discourage investment in new enterprises. New Zealand has also failed to develop advanced manufactured goods or electronic products that can compete on world markets. Currently it lags far behind Australia in industrial development. But while its economic prospects remain uncertain, New Zealand is aggressively promoting its timber resources, fisheries, and tourist industry.

Year-Round Tourism

Tourists come to New Zealand year-round because it has four distinct and very pleasant seasons. Summer has plenty of sunshine, and in and on the water visitors enjoy such activities as snorkeling, rafting, kayaking, and scuba diving. Golfing, hiking, fishing, hunting, and camping are also popular summer sports. Watching geysers erupt is a popular pastime at the Rotorua thermal area on North Island. According to Maori legend, Hinemoa, forbidden to visit her lover from another tribe, swam across Lake Rotorua to the island where he lived. Upon the discovery of the couple, the tribes celebrated her demonstration of love, and the hostility between the tribes ended. Rotorua was first discovered 600 years ago by a Maori explorer named Ihenga. He was out hunting when one of his dogs disappeared while chasing a kiwi. The dog later returned home with a wet coat and had apparently eaten a meal of fish. Ihenga realized that he must be near water, so he searched until he found Lake Rotoiti and later, Rotorua. Rotorua is known for its colorful pools, boiling mud, and erupting geysers, which have the sulfurous odor of rotten eggs. Whakarewarewa is a major site of geothermal activity and also the major seat of Maori culture. Tourists can watch Maori artisans polishing gems or carving wood there.

Mount Tarawera is one of many volcanoes in this area. The 1886 eruption of Tarawera killed 153 people and destroyed the White and Pink Terraces, huge silica formations that were then New Zealand's most famous tourist attraction. From the 3,644-foot (1,110-meter) summit you can see White Island, a volcano smoking in the Bay of Plenty nearly 70 miles (43.5 kilometers) away. Tourists can hike the volcanoes or go whitewater rafting on the Kaituna, Rangitaiki, and Wairoa Rivers. The Kaituna River offers the highest waterfalls in the world that the adventurous can take a raft over. The plunge over the falls is a drop of 22 feet (6.7 meters) in rushing water.

During the winter months, New Zealand's climate is mild and temperatures usually do not fall below freezing in the lowlands. In the mountains, winter snowfall provides excellent skiing conditions. Some tourists enjoy more active vacations and trek the trails on South Island. Abel

The 1886 eruption of Mount Tarawera near Rotomahana destroyed the White and Pink Terraces, which at that time were the most famous tourist attraction in New Zealand.

Tasman, Heaphy, and Queen Charlotte Sounds Walkway are trails located at the northernmost part of South Island. These trails can be walked year-round. However, trails at higher elevations such as the world-famous Milford Track, Kepler, and Routeburn are closed in the winter due to snow

Whale watching has become a rapidly growing activity around the world, and New Zealand is a leader in establishing rules and codes of conduct that govern whale watching. The sleepy little town of Kaikoura is located on South Island, and whales have made it a tourist attraction. A century ago whalers nearly wiped out the sperm-whale population; now the town depends on the whale for its survival. Tourists pour into the town's emerald-green harbor to go out on whale-watching boats.

Whales are the world's largest mammals (the sperm whale is the largest of the toothed whales). They are difficult to spot because they spend six minutes underwater for every minute they spend on the surface. When they come up for air, they often spout and roll around until they are ready to plunge back into the depths. Schools of bottlenose dolphins often frolic by the hundreds in the foamy wake of the whales. New techniques have recently been developed that allow researchers to tally the whales in an area and determine how long they stay underwater by counting and tracking the "clicks," or sounds, they make underwater.

Foreign Investment

Increasingly, New Zealand has been forging important ties with its neighbors around the Pacific Rim. New Zealand and Australia are both members of the 18-member Asia-Pacific Economic Cooperation (APEC) group. In 1995 this group agreed to establish "free and open" trade and investment between member states by the year 2020.

These hikers on Fox Glacier are exploring the terrain of one of the world's few advancing glaciers.

Approximately one-half of all companies doing business in New Zealand are based in Australia. Almost 20 per cent of New Zealand's largest 100 corporations are actually controlled by Australians. This trend is especially prevalent in the financial sector. Seventy percent of New Zealand's banking assets are managed by Australian institutions. Recent economic reforms have even allowed the Bank of New Zealand to be bought out by the National Australia Bank. Meanwhile, Australian mass-media magazines, movies, and television programs continue to flood New Zealand's market. These trends are making New Zealanders very uneasy and nervous because they see Australians buying out New Zealand interests and moving corporate headquarters across the Tasman Sea to Australia. This triggers job losses and removes New Zealanders from important business decisions. As multinational corporations move into the area, they consistently prefer to set up their offices in Australia and not New Zealand. New Zealand's stock market is predicted to merge soon with Australia's. Following that union, some critics predict a single Australian-dominated currency will follow. Today over 20 per cent of New Zealand's imports and exports come from Australia, and the pattern of regional free trade will probably strengthen in the future.

Japan's influence on the country is also a concern. Though aware of Japan's economic strength and its potential for benefiting their own country through joint ventures, loans, and trade, some New Zealanders worry that Japanese wealth may symbolize the decline of New Zealand's unique culture. They are afraid that Japan may use its spending power to unduly influence and affect the culture of New Zealanders. For example, Japanese tourists began visiting New Zealand in vast numbers during the 1980s; however, many of them complained about the quality of the country's hotels. New Zealand could not come up with the funds to upgrade its hotels, so they accepted Japan's offer to build new hotels themselves. New Zealanders believed that their construction industry, as well as their economy as a whole, would benefit from Japan's investment. They also felt that wealthy Japanese tourists might be inclined to visit more often and spend more money if luxury hotels were available. They hoped that the upgrading of tourist amenities would boost tourism.

In 1999 a traditional Maori war dance, or *haka,* greeted a group of foreign dignitaries at Auckland Airport.

8

New Zealand Looks Ahead

N ew Zealanders face many challenges. One of the most pressing is that of Maori claims to land. Recent protests include periodic civic disobedience, growing Maori land claims over much of North and South Islands, and a call to return the country's name to the indigenous "Aotearoa." In response, the government has increased Maori land and fishing rights and proposed a series of financial and land settlements that are under consideration by the Maori.

New Zealanders are trying to rectify the historic discrimination of unfair treaties that had been put in place by their forbearers. Parliament now includes several Maori members. In the 1990s, the Labour/ Green Party coalition tried to put behind some of the antiquated colonial remnants by eliminating knighthoods bestowed by the British Crown. Instead of knighthoods, local honors are awarded.

When Queen Elizabeth II visited New Zealand in 1995 to celebrate the 150-year anniversary of the Treaty of Waitangi, some protestors gave her a less than warm welcome.

New Zealand's economic prospects are uncertain at this point. Its growth-oriented economic strategy may pay off in the future, although the 1990s were a decade of economic stagnation for New Zealand. Since 1984 the government has accomplished major economic restructuring by moving an agrarian economy toward a free market, a more industrialized economy that can compete globally. This dynamic growth

Sculpting beautiful designs in wood has been a traditional Maori art form for centuries.

has boosted real incomes, broadened and deepened its technological capabilities, and put a damper on inflation. Per capita gross national income has been rising toward that of the Western European countries. New Zealand's heavy dependence on trade makes its growth prospects vulnerable to economic performance in Asia, Australia, Europe, and the United States. Because of its dependence of foreign trade, New Zealand strives to maintain good relations with many countries.

The widening income gap between the wealthy and the poor threatens to undermine New Zealand's social foundation.

A sculpture of a kiwi, New Zealand's national bird, stands in Queenstown.

While city dwellers prosper from the recent economic reforms, the country's rural populations continue to struggle as the markets for their agricultural products decline.

Both the Maori and the white New Zealanders worry about the superior financial strength of the Japanese and newly industrializing Asian and Southeast Asian peoples who they fear may diminish their own culture in some way. The Maori have complained recently about Japanese net fishing and its damage to its own fishing industry. Historically, the Maori have often had to submit to those who would impose their will and rule over them, but the white New Zealanders are not used to such accommodation and may have a difficult time adjusting to this situation.

No matter what the future holds for New Zealand, it will continue to be a land of rare beauty. The people—bound in a culture that fuses European with Maori ancestry—are friendly, helpful, and extremely resourceful.

Facts at a Glance

Land and People

Official Name of Country	New Zealand
Location	Oceania, islands in the South Pacific Ocean, southeast of Australia
Area	268,670 square kilometers
Highest Point	Mount Cook 3,764 meters
Lowest Point	Pacific Ocean 0 meters
Capital	Wellington
Other Major Cities	Auckland, Christchurch, Hamilton
Terrain	Predominantly mountainous with some large coastal plains
Climate	Temperate to subtropical with sharp regional contrasts
Population	4,000,000 (July 2000 est.)
Official Language	English
Other Major Languages	Maori
Ethnic Groups	New Zealand European 74.5%, Maori 9.7%, other European 4.6%, Pacific Islander 3.8%, Asian and others 7.4%
Literacy Rate	99% (1980 est.)
Religions	Anglican 24%, Prebyterian 18%, Roman Catholic 15%, Methodist 5%, Baptist 2%, other Protestant 3%, unspecified or none 33%
Average Life Expectancy	78.5 years

Economy

Natural Resources	Natural gas, iron ore, sand, coal, timber, hydropower, gold, limestone
Land Use	Arable: 9%, permanent crops 5%, permanent pastures 50%, forests and woodland 28%, other 8%.
Major Exports	Food, wood and paper products, wool, textiles, dairy products, iron and steel
Major Imports	Machinery, equipment, vehicles, aircraft, petroleum, consumer goods, plastics
Major Trading Partners	Australia, Japan, United States
Currency	New Zealand dollar

Government

Form of Government	Parliamentary democracy
Legislature	Unicameral House of Representatives called Parliament
Political Party	Many
Head of Government	Prime Minister Helen Clark (since December 10, 1999)
Head of State	Queen Elizabeth II (since February 6, 1952)
Voting Rights	Universal suffrage at age 18 years
Constitution	No formal, written constitution; consists of various legal documents

950 A.D.	Polynesians reach New Zealand
1000	Moa hunters visit islands regularly
1350s	Maoris, probably from Tahiti, settle the islands
1642	New Zealand is "discovered" by Dutch navigator Abel J. Tasman
1769	Captain James Cook explores the islands
1840s	British begin to settle islands and Britain declares sovereignty
1865	A gold rush attracts new immigrants
1907	New Zealand becomes an almost independent dominion of Great Britain
1941	Socialized medicine is implemented
1947	New Zealand becomes fully independent within the British Commonwealth of Nations; New Zealand backs creation of the South Pacific Commission
1950s	Export markets restructured
1970s	The National Party takes power; New Zealand foregoes foreign policy more independent of traditional allies
1980s	The Labour Party regains power; New Zealand withdraws from ANZUS
1990s	New Zealanders consider withdrawing from the Commonwealth; Maoris and white New Zealanders face economic challenges from other nations of the Pacific Rim
2000s	New Zealand is led by its second woman prime minister, Helen Clark; the nation champions cultural and environmental goals; Parliament debates the merits of a proposed parent-leave law

Further Reading

Cockerton, Camilla. "Women." In *The Pacific Islands: Environment and Society*, ed. Moshe Rapaport. Honolulu: Bess Press, 1999, pp. 305–314.

Cumberland, Kenneth B. *Southwest Pacific: A Geography of Australia, New Zealand, and Their Pacific Island Neighborhoods.* Christchurch: Whitcomb and Tombs, 1968.

Hall, Colin M. *Tourism in the Pacific Rim.* New York: John Wiley & Sons, 1994.

McKnight, Tom L. *The Geography of Australia, New Zealand, and the Pacific Islands.* Englewood Cliffs, N.J.: Prentice Hall, 1995.

Pawson, Eric. "Two New Zealands: Maori and European." In *Inventing Places*, ed. Kay Anderson and Fay Gale. Melbourne: Longman Cheshire, 1992.

Bradshaw, Michael. *The New Global Order: World Regional Geography,* 2nd ed. New York: McGraw- Hill, 2001.

English, Paul. *Geography: People and Places in a Changing World,* 2nd ed. St. Paul, Minn.: West Publishing, 1997.

Rainbow, Stephen. *Green Politics.* New York: Oxford University Press, 1994.

Rice, Geoffrey W. *The Oxford History of New Zealand.* New York: Oxford University Press, 1993.

Sager, Robert J., and David Helgren. *World Geography Today.* New York: Holt, Rinehart, and Winston, 1997.

Salter, Christopher, et al. *Essentials of World Regional Geography,* 3rd ed. Orlando, Fla.: Saunders College Publishing, 2000.

Index

Index

Frontispiece: Flag courtesy of *www.theodora.com/flags* used with permission

page:

About the Author

CAROL ANN GILLESPIE teaches World Regional Geography and East Asian Studies at Grove City College in Grove City, Pennsylvania. She resides in Cranberry Township, PA with her husband, Michael, and her three sons. She enjoys travel and is currently writing a geography-based adventure series for young readers.

CHARLES F. ("FRITZ") GRITZNER is Distinguished Professor of Geography at South Dakota University in Brookings. He is now in his fifth decade of college teaching and research. During his career, he has taught more than 60 different courses, spanning the fields of physical, cultural, and regional geography. In addition to his teaching, he enjoys writing, working with teachers, and sharing his love for geography with students. As consulting editor for the MODERN WORLD NATIONS series, he has a wonderful opportunity to combine all of these "hobbies." Fritz has served as both President and Executive Director of the National Council for Geographic Education and has received the Council's highest honor, the George J. Miller Award for Distinguished Service. In March 2004, he won the Distinguished Teaching award from the American Association of Geographers at their annual meeting held in Philadelphia.